THEODOR FÜRCHTEGOTT KIRCHNER
NEW SCENES OF CHILDHOOD
Op.55

Edited by Lionel Salter

The very title of this album proclaims Theodor Kirchner (1823–1903) as a disciple of Schumann, whom he met when he went to study in Leipzig in 1838 (which was also the year of Schumann's own *Scenes of Childhood*). Kirchner had been a precociously gifted organist, and his playing so impressed Mendelssohn that he recommended the not yet 20-year-old youth for the post of organist in Winterthur (Switzerland), where he took a leading part in the town's musical life and won the admiration of Liszt and Wagner (some of whose rehearsals he accompanied). After twenty years there, he moved to Zurich, where he was active for a decade as a conductor; but he then became increasingly restless, spending a year as music master to the Princess Amalie, then directing the new music school in Würzburg, and teaching successively in Leipzig, Dresden and Hamburg, where he died.

He wrote an immense number of short piano pieces in the tradition of Schumann, marked by polished craftsmanship and nearly all, despite their simplicity, containing unexpected touches. The present album was first published in Berlin in 1881.

LIONEL SALTER
London, 1985

THE ASSOCIATED BOARD OF
THE ROYAL SCHOOLS OF MUSIC

£1·80

NEW SCENES OF CHILDHOOD

1

Allegretto [♩ = 108]

KIRCHNER, Op. 55

2

3

4

Andantino espressivo [♪ = 138]

5

6

Poco vivace [♩ = 112]

7

Start 22nd Sav.

8

Allegretto [♩ = 112]

9

10

11

12

13

Skarl 25th Man

14

Nicht schnell [Non allegro] [♩ = 104] **15**

Start Tues 26h

16

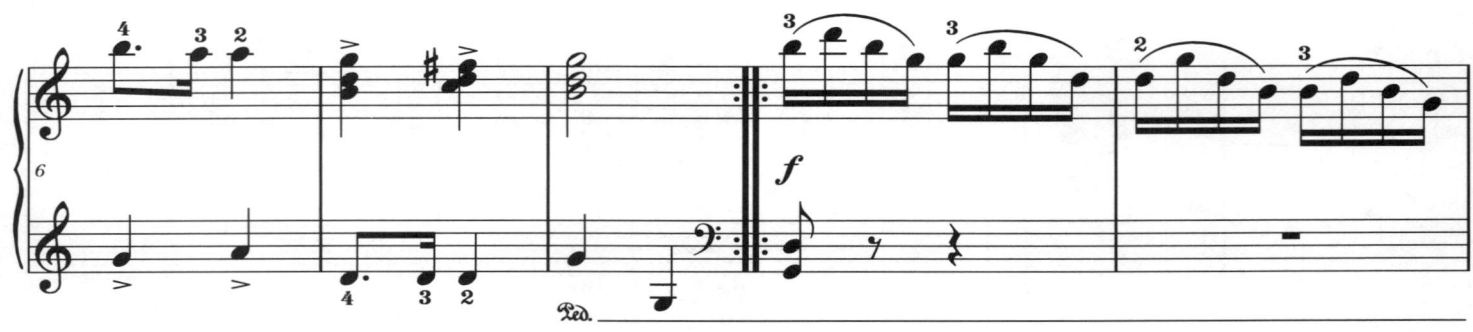

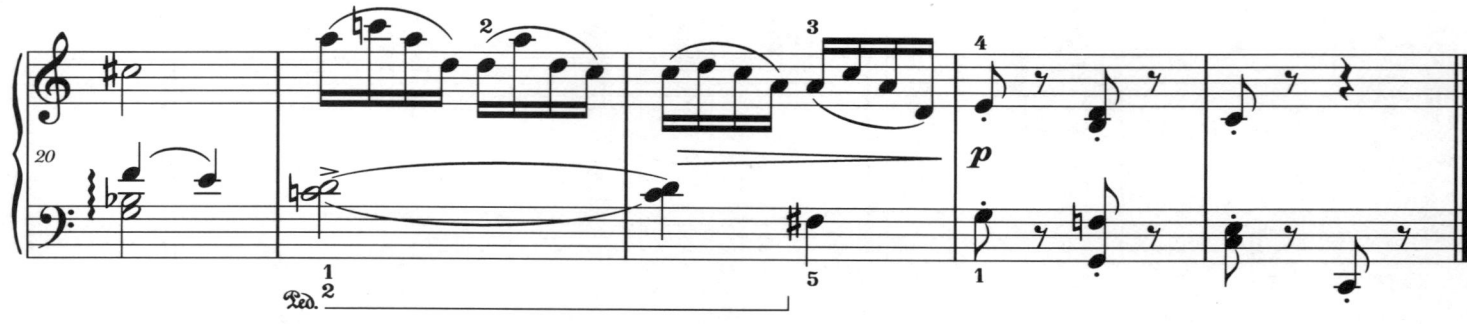

17

Ruhig [Tranquillo] [♩ = 96]

18

Skart Wed 27/2

19

Poco vivace [♩.= 69]

20

21

Start Thurs. 28th

22

23

24

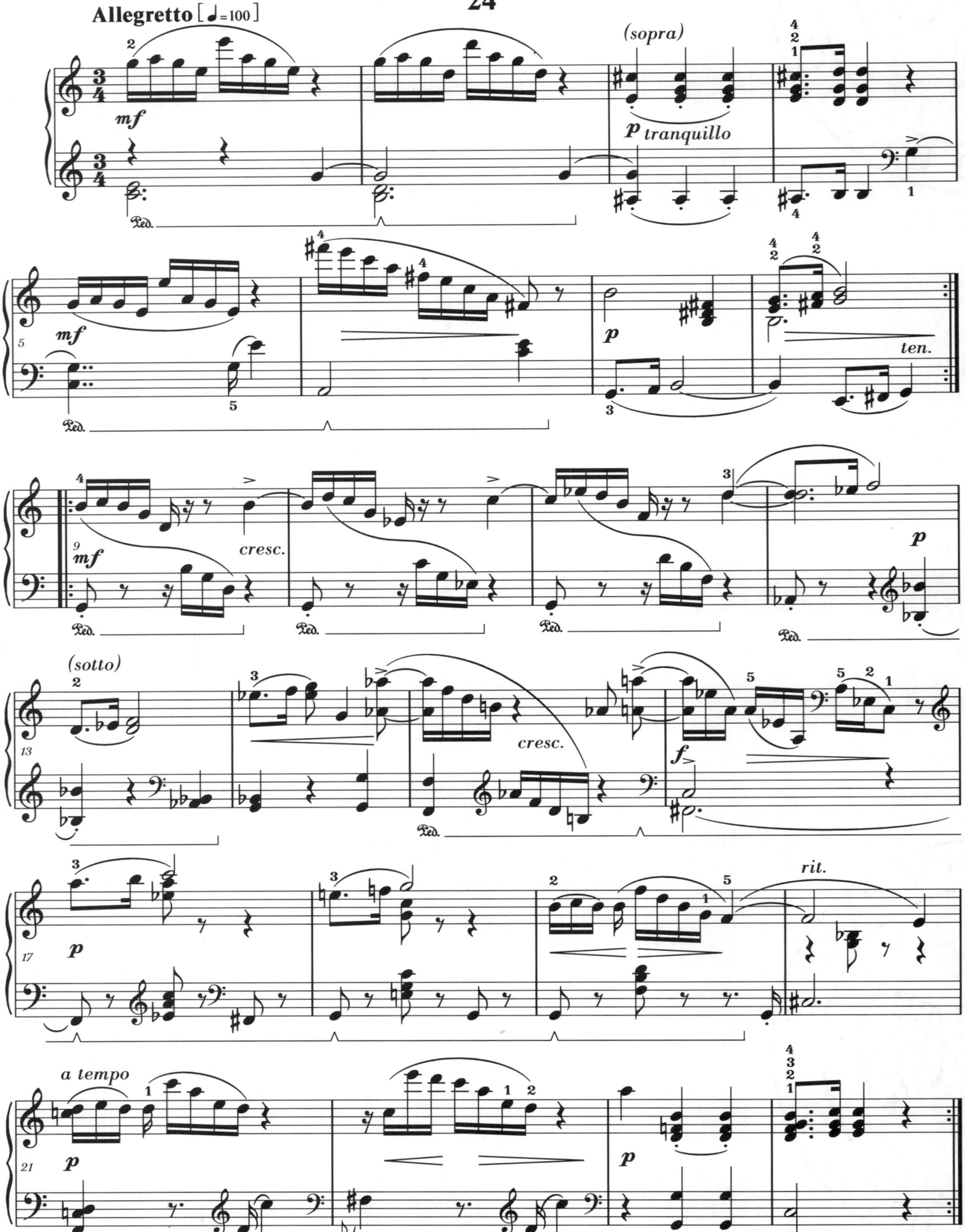
Allegretto [♩=100]
mf
Ped.
(sopra)
p tranquillo
mf
p
ten.
mf
cresc.
p
(sotto)
cresc.
f
p
rit.
a tempo
p
p

25

AB 1912

Reproduced and printed by
Halstan & Co. Ltd., Amersham, Bucks., England